Series Editor - Sylvia P. Webb

Sylvia Webb is a well known consultant, author and lecturer in the information management field. Her first book 'Creating an Information Service' was published by Aslib and has sold in over forty countries. She has experience of working in both the public and private sectors, ranging from public libraries to national and international organisations. She has also been a lecturer at Ashridge Management College, specialising in management and inter-personal skills, which led to her second book, 'Personal Development in Information Work', also published by Aslib. She has served on a number of government advisory bodies, is actively involved in professional education with Aslib and the Library Association and is also a former Vice-President of the Institute of Information Scientists. As well as being editor of this series, Sylvia Webb has also written two of the Know How guides; 'Making a charge for Library and Information Services', and 'Preparing a guide to your library and information service'.

A list of titles in the Aslib Know How Series
appears on the back cover of this volume.

Contents

1. Introduction

Guides to library and information services (LIS) come in an ever-increasing variety of shapes, sizes and formats. Widely-available and easy-to-use graphics software and desk top publishing facilities have certainly contributed to this. So has the increased awareness among LIS professionals of the potential of a well-produced and up-to-date guide in promoting the service and ensuring that maximum use is made of its facilities. LIS guides can range from a single sheet of A4 paper to videos and interactive computer-based packages. Printed versions might be presented as a simple bookmark or a reference card, or as a more comprehensive brochure, booklet or information pack. A number of the printed versions (and other formats) are produced in-house, whilst some are printed and produced commercially. This sometimes involves the use of design consultants and external printers, and can result in some visually impressive glossy brochures and alternative products.

Often there is not just a single guide to the service, but a series of separate sources of information on different aspects of, or specific services within the overall LIS. These can be issued individually or in a specially designed folder which may be given to all new users, providing them with a guide to the total service. Guides may also be planned and prepared to be used in conjunction with, or to supplement oral presentations and guided tours of the LIS. Rather than being purely descriptive, these could well include practical exercises to assist the user in gaining an appreciation of the content, arrangement and use of information sources. This is increasingly the case in academic LIS where the new student may well be expected to use specific sources as part of the learning process (see the section on subject guides in Chapter 3).

So is there any one way, to be preferred above all others, in which to produce a successful and effective guide to your service? The answer, as could have been expected from the above comments, is definitely 'no', but there are a number of matters to be taken into account, and questions addressed before you set out on the path towards producing your next guide. Perhaps, up to now, in your LIS there has been no guide, or any which has existed is now either out-of-date in terms of content, or in terms of style, or both. What are the key considerations for the LIS manager or other member of staff who is thinking about producing or updating a guide to the service?

A useful starting point could be to consider the questions which you might ask in producing any written report - they apply equally well to other formats. These are the oft-quoted, but still extremely pertinent, "six honest serving men" featured in Kipling's poem "I keep six honest serving men". They are What, Why, When, How, Where and Who? In applying them, although in a different order, to the development of a library guide we would be seeking answers to the following initial questions:

- WHY have a guide; what is its purpose; what do we hope that it will achieve; does it have a long-term as well as a short-term aim; could it help fulfil any other aims; where does it fit into both organisational and departmental objectives?

- WHAT do we want to say i.e. dependent on the stated purpose what needs to be included; which particular features or aspects of the service do we want to describe; how much detail is required?

- WHO is the perceived reader/user at whom the guide is aimed - the intended audience; is there more than one identifiable user or potential user group; what implication does this have for decisions on content and style?

- HOW should we present the information in the guide; given the make-up of the potential user group or groups, what level and language style should we adopt; what format should be used - paper, electronic or other; who is going to write the text and have overall responsibility for its production: what about design details like size, shape and colour; is there a house style to which we need to conform; should we design an appropriate logo for the LIS to make the guide instantly recognisable; should it be produced internally or externally; if it is not to be a printed guide what would be the most appropriate format; what supporting equipment might be needed?

- WHERE is it intended to be used; what access (local or remote) will there be to the guide; how widely will it be made available; what implications does this have for LIS space and equipment e.g. siting of terminals for a computer-based package, or control systems for loan copies to be used off-site, or viewing facilities for a video-based guide; what impact does the place where it is used have on the number of copies which may be required?

- WHEN is it likely to be used; is it intended to be an 'in-hand' guide which can only be used within the physical confines of the LIS as an aid to locating and making use of material; what implications are there for the hours of opening and staffing levels; if it is intended to be used on a network, will it be accessible at all times and are users then able to conveniently follow-up their requirements; does it act as an introduction which new users need to read before visiting or making contact with the LIS; is there follow-up material which needs to be studied at specific future points in time in relation to particular scheduled usage e.g. as part of a programme of training or an education syllabus?

These suggested initial considerations indicate just how much planning is required in producing a guide if it is to be really effective in achieving its objectives. Answers to questions under any one of the above headings are likely to influence those under another. For example, questions about format under HOW will also relate to those on access and equipment under WHERE. All the answers will lead to further questions which will have to be addressed, for example, in relation to resourcing, is there a budget available for the development of a guide; if so, will there also be money available in the future for updating and change; what are the implications for staff time, not just in terms of producing the guide, but also in meeting the expectations of users which may have been engendered by the guide; are there implications for staff training and development in terms of acquiring or upgrading certain areas of skill and knowledge?

The act of carrying out the initial planning of the guide should not be viewed as an isolated task, it needs to be considered as part of the overall strategy for disseminating information about, and promoting the services and skills available within and through the LIS, in other words part of the LIS public relations and marketing policy. For example, it should be coordinated with any plans for signposting, labelling and guiding to assist users in finding their way around the physical layout and arrangement of the LIS. It is also likely to have wider repercussions in terms of suggesting possible changes and future directions for the service, so it can play a positive and constructive role in broader management planning.

3

2. Why produce a guide?

Establishing the need

As indicated in the previous chapter, before making a decision about style or presentation, you will need to have a clearly-stated purpose for the guide. Why is it thought to be necessary and what does it hope to achieve? In order to answer these questions it could be useful to go back to the *raison d'être* of the LIS itself - what is it there to do, what does it currently offer, what additional or alternative services could it provide? That in turn suggests looking at the current objectives of the parent organisation and its future direction. If, as in the case of an academic library, it is part of an institution with education and research objectives, then the LIS objectives will be developed in support of, and relate strongly to those objectives. Equally in a special library or information centre, although the role and objectives of the LIS may be different to those of its counterparts in public or academic libraries, they must relate just as strongly to those of the parent organisation as a whole.

The size of the organisation and the spread of its activities, both in terms of its fields of interest and operation, and the number and location of sites to be served, will also play a part in determining the purpose and style of any guide to the LIS. It is generally accepted that however large or small the organisation may be, if the LIS is to maximise its usefulness it needs to ensure that users and potential users are made aware not only of its existence and its current services, but also its possible wider contribution in achieving corporate objectives. A simple LIS guide can certainly help in this. In referring to the importance of producing "leaflets and brochures which advertise the services and resources of your library or information unit" Hamilton (1990) says "It doesn't matter if you are working in a tiny one-room, one-staff operation, or a large, many-floored, many-branched organisation with a staff of hundreds, the production of such material will be essential".

Awards for good PR material

Each year in the United Kingdom a series of awards is made to promote and improve the standards of public relations and publicity within library and information services. These are known as the Library Association/T C Farries Public Relations & Publicity Awards and attract hundreds of entries annually across the various categories, covering public relations programmes, special events, publicity material, sponsorship and partnership funding, and personal PR achievement. Category 3 (Publicity Material), which cover posters, handout publicity, any single publication for sale, and audiovisual materials, is the one in which LIS guides are submitted, unless they form part of a planned programme of good PR practice. There has been a lot of interest in producing audiovisual material and the CD-ROM format has also featured in this category.

The judges for the awards look for:

* excellence, imagination and innovation in the promotion of library and information services

* presentation to complement the standard of the entry itself

* supporting information clearly presented.

The enthusiasm of entrants and the increase in the number of entries indicates the importance now attached not only to informing users of what is available in their LIS, but also of how to do this as professionally as possible.

Preparing your LIS guide will give you the opportunity to consider afresh the services which you offer. The expectations of LIS users or clients concerning services and methods of delivery must be taken into account. If there has been any recent survey of user/customer needs, or of the level of satisfaction with the overall service and its constituent parts, then any possible changes which might come about in response to those expressions of satisfaction or need will have to be built into your plans for the guide.

So the planning of something as seemingly simple as a guide to the LIS could involve asking some searching questions about where we are and where we are going. This is particularly the case when the LIS has only recently been established, or has undergone radical change and development. Even when the LIS is long-established it can be well worthwhile 'revisiting' the organisation as a whole, making sure that you are up to date with current developments. For example, if the organisation is planning any quality initiatives such as introducing a Total Quality Management policy or setting up a customer charter, this could have a considerable impact on what you offer and the way in which this should be presented in any user guide. Whether or not any dramatic organisational change is planned it would still be appropriate to review the LIS and its range of services. Before you start preparing a guide, you need to be as sure as you can be that what you are going to describe i.e. the services and their arrangement and delivery, are likely to continue to be relevant and to be offered in the same way. The LIS often forms part of another function such as Research or Marketing and in this case there will be an additional dimension to consider, that of the overall departmental objectives in relation to those of the organisation.

This review and 'revisiting' can prove extremely useful in providing a new focus for considering the appropriateness of your service and will stimulate new thinking on methods of information provision. It provides the opportunity to consult further with users and learn more about their information needs, at the same time involving LIS staff in the process, which can have a significant effect on their job satisfaction and motivation. It can bring to light a range of staff skills and knowledge which might hitherto have been overlooked or under-utilised. Advice on, and discussion of ways of getting to know the organisation and appropriately developing the LIS is set out in much more detail in *Creating an Information Service*, (Webb, 1988).

Having done your own background research on the above, this should help in establishing the different needs of your users in terms of the information which they are likely to require about the service and the way in which it operates. It will sharpen up or perhaps reaffirm your ideas for a guide or series of guides, but above all it will clarify the purpose of the guide - what it is setting out to achieve.

3. Purpose and coverage of different types of guide

General promotion

The overall purpose of any guide is to inform, but about what and in which manner will vary considerably. There will be as much variation in purpose as in style and presentation. Whatever the stated intention, from informing users of the hours of opening or the charges made for photocopying, to guiding thcm through specific source material, all guides additionally will serve the purpose of promoting the LIS. This must therefore be at the forefront of thinking throughout the preparation of the guide. Often the overriding purpose will be one of promotion. This is particularly true where a new library or information service has been set up or when radical changes to the service have taken place, especially those affecting availability, delivery methods, or the client base. There will also be an ongoing need for the regular publicising of existing services. The client who today does not have a need for certain information, may well require it in the future. Even the most frequent users of the overall service may well need to be constantly reminded of the full range of services available, as well as being made aware of new ones.

There will be a number of different situations or policies which could provide an opportunity to promote the LIS and which could lead to the production of various sorts of guide. These might be intended to be of a brief and temporary nature just to get the message across as quickly as possible, or to become longer term standard guides.

Examples of policies and situations which could be used in this way are as follows:

- as part of continuous user contact

- to introduce additional or upgraded services

- to inform of operational changes e.g. loan arrangements, the introduction of fee-based services, the availability of certain services via the organisational computer network

- to provide information on LIS staff such as contact details, subject specialisms, changes

- to publicise demonstrations or special events.

7

These are just some of the many possible examples; you will be able to add more, but the key point is that they all bring with them an opportunity to remind existing users of, and alert new and potential users to the LIS and what it can offer. Each of the above suggested areas could form the basis for a brochure which builds around the specific item other relevant information which would be of interest to a particular user group. If you take the last one on the above list, you might want to inform people of a demonstration of a new database. Rather than just issuing an invitation with details of time, date and venue, you could also refer to other databases or related source material, along with brief descriptions of coverage and availability. A tear-off form could be added so that you will be able not only to assess interest in the demonstration, but also obtain wider feedback regarding the potential usage of, and interest in the subject area or the format. The event itself will also act as a promotion opportunity and the way in which it is organised and conducted should be seen as an integral part of your overall publicity strategy and as such will influence the preparation process of any related literature. If you promote the event by email you may wish to make similar information available for screen consultation, in which case its style and presentation will be very different to that of a printed guide, although it will have the same purpose. The appropriateness of different ways of presenting the information are discussed further in Chapter 6.

Location and access

Perhaps the most basic but essential and therefore widely produced type of guide, is the one which provides details of where the LIS is situated, the easiest way of getting to it and accessing the building. This has the simple purpose of getting people to the right place at the right time and by the most direct and convenient means. It will have a small amount of text giving essential details such as the hours of opening, with a note of staff names and contact numbers, and sometimes a short description in words of the location. However by far the clearest way to indicate this is to incorporate a map showing where it is in relation to the rest of the site, and if it is part of a large organisation, where the site is in relation to nearby named main streets, or to the city centre and bus, underground or rail stations.

If the LIS covers several buildings, or a number of floors or levels of a single building, you will need to show which broad subject areas and which particular facilities are located in a specific building or on a particular floor. Visitors will need to know exactly where the cloakrooms and refreshment facilities can be found, as well as where the online terminals or photocopiers are situated. Buildings need to be labelled on the map and the numbers or letters indicating floors or levels shown. Main entrances and exits should be clearly marked, especially emergency exits. The location of staircases, escalators and lifts should be indicated, with clear reference to wheelchair access. Goods entrances, which often have large capacity lifts for the transport of heavy or bulky goods, should also be shown. You might well be sending this guide out to a new supplier, or to other occasional visitors, as well as to regular and long-term users of the LIS, so make sure that all these eventualities are covered.

Layout

Having successfully guided your visitors to the LIS, the entrance to which must be clearly marked itself so that they know that they have actually arrived at the right place, what will now be required is more detail about what is inside. Visitors will require answers to questions about where specific sections or services are to be found e.g. where are the economics journals, or the company annual reports; where are the enquiry points and the individual staff who will be able to advise; is there a single photocopying area or are there a number of machines located at various points around the LIS, perhaps for each subject area; are the online facilities situated with their relevant subject areas or grouped together in a separate section? If, for example, users have got as far as the social sciences floor, where within it can they track down their specific requirements among the various different fields which fall within that broad discipline; where can they consult the catalogue or other listings which will help them in this?

The purpose of your next guide will be to address those questions, by means of drawing up a detailed plan of the layout, showing the precise location of each subject area, labelling each section with both a verbal description e.g. Vocational Education, and its classification code, 370.113 if you are using the Dewey Decimal Classification Scheme. The plan should point out where the book stock is located, and where journals and other material, both print and non-print, can be found. More detailed guides to specific subjects can be produced separately and are described later, but at this stage the user should be able to follow the plan to whatever subject areas or facilities may be required, with the route between them clearly set out, showing adjoining or linking corridors, staircases and lifts, and again indicating appropriate entrances and exits to particular rooms or areas. It is also worth repeating the indication of cloakrooms and refreshment facilities, as already described in the general location guide, if these are available within, or close to specific areas shown on the more detailed LIS layout plan.

Individual floors, rooms and other separate sections need to be clearly marked themselves in order to be quickly and easily recognisable from whatever labelling you put on the plan. It is no good showing 'The Mozart Room' on your plan of the music library, if the room itself has an unmarked entrance. Therefore in order to be most helpful, you will need to check what signs and labels are in place, where additional ones or replacements may be required, and design the guide to the layout of the LIS with these in mind.

Operational details

This guide, or this part of your complete guide if it is to be produced as one package, has as its purpose the introduction of the user to the ways in which the service runs and how material or information can be traced and made available. This is the 'what you need to do if you want....' section. It will cover the way in which the service as a whole operates, as well as providing information on individual operations within it, for example, on the use of the online catalogue, or how to carry out bibliographic searching. However with the two examples just given it is envisaged that reference would be made in the guide to the more detailed instructions displayed beside the machine as discussed later. Bibliographic searching could also form part of a subject guide and the examples drawn from the particular field of interest.

The guide will provide general descriptions of the different ways in which to trace material and how it may be obtained from other sources if not available in-house. The system for requesting and purchasing material and the ordering and control of subscriptions, which in a number of private sector and other organisations is carried out centrally by the LIS, should also be outlined. Where charges made for LIS services are passed on to individual departmental budgets, the system and procedures for doing this should be described.

The operational guide will describe the use and control of reference material and electronic sources such as CD-ROM and online databases. Information on who can use the LIS, different categories of membership if these exist, how to join and of course the benefits of being a member will be set out here. Details of the loan system will be required - how it works, whether borrowers need cards, how many books can be borrowed, whether the loan system is extended to other material such as journals, video- and audio-cassettes, CDs, and what restrictions there are, for example, different loan periods for different types of material such as short-term loans of textbooks in academic libraries. In many special libraries there are few restrictions, either on the length of time for which an item may be borrowed, or on the loan of journals or so-called 'reference books' - rather there is a preference, but most things are negotiable. However that does not stop you putting some sort of guideline into any published LIS guide; at least it provides the user with an idea of what is 'best practice' and gives you a starting point for negotiation. There may well be no readers' tickets or cards, the loan system may work on a 'self-service' basis, with the user completing some sort of record when an item is removed from the LIS. This is often the case where the LIS is open on a twenty four hour basis, but not staffed throughout. Users still need to know how the system operates, whether they can have access to material in the absence of LIS staff, and whether there are any preferences for certain items to be used in the LIS whenever possible. In a corporate library, material which has been borrowed will probably be staying in the building anyway, its use in most cases being in relation to a specific work-related activity being carried out in-house.

The operational guide should cover the other standard procedures of which the user needs to be aware, such as photocopying and copyright restrictions; any charges made such as those for photocopies, or for fines, or to cover inter-library loan costs. If there is a booking system for the use of terminals or audio-visual material that should be described. You also need to include a note of any study facilities available such as a reading room or study area.

Rather than putting in the guide detailed descriptions of procedures relating to the use of a specific piece of equipment it is often more helpful to present these at the point of use. For example, straightforward instructions in the form of a clear and obvious notice placed beside a computer terminal, will be of much more use to the user than a section within a general guide which covers a range of other procedures. Initially it is also likely to be more directly helpful than the often large and not necessarily easy-to-use technical manuals which may accompany the system. Before making use of the system, the only information that the user needs is how to get into it, so a clearly written notice or set of instructions is vital. Once in the system, given that the majority of computer-based packages in use in the LIS will be menu-driven, the user will find that using it is likely to be self-explanatory. That is not to suggest that the manuals are not required or should not be available. They are an essential part of the more detailed portfolio of instructions to which both users and LIS staff need to have access and as such could be located on a shelf near the terminal for reference as required, or made available on request if they are likely to be infrequently used by enquirers.

A similar approach could be taken in relation to the use of the catalogue, which may be computer-based, in microfiche form, or available wholly or in part in printed form. When preparing a guide to the use of the catalogue, clear and concise instructions are again best placed at the point of use. In the case of a computerised catalogue, even though the introduction to its use will probably be written into the software, there is still a case for a short note about its use to be displayed beside the terminal.

The above are just two examples of the way in which an individual operation or procedure can be explained or described to the user simply and to greatest effect. As mentioned earlier in relation to the guide to the LIS layout, it highlights the importance of preparing your operations guide with all LIS signposting and labelling in mind. If it is designed to be complementary to, and used in conjunction with signing and guiding around the individual sections of the LIS, it can play a key part in your overall strategy which aims to get the user to the required information or material as quickly and easily as possible.

Safety and security regulations and procedures must be clearly set out e.g. restrictions on what may be brought into the LIS; emergency action to be taken in the case of fire; smoking or non-smoking regulations. If there are restrictions, for example, on taking coats or bags into the LIS area, then information on cloakroom provision should also be included here. There is likely to be an overall organisational requirement for safety and security procedures to be clearly displayed around the building, so make sure that you have got the latest information for your guide, although notes of any changes should have been circulated to all staff as a matter of course. There should also be named safety officers for each part of the building, so it could be a good idea to discuss this part of the guide with them, and include a name and contact details, even if this is a member of LIS staff and their details appear elsewhere in connection with other duties.

Subject guides

The purpose of a subject guide is to introduce the enquirer or any potential user to the range and type of material within a given field and to assist them in making an informed choice of the source most appropriate to meeting their specific need. The subject guide also aims to help users to become aware of the arrangement and retrieval procedures related to the use of particular types of material within their field of interest and through this to gain an appreciation of how they can make the most of those different sources. For both these reasons they are likely to include descriptions of key sources, indicating their coverage and content, arrangement and use, potential usefulness for particular purposes, and availability and access. If they are prepared in relation to a specific syllabus or course, lists of recommended reading and practical exercises may be included.

A subject guide will usually repeat some of the information already presented in the other types of guides already mentioned, especially those on location and layout. If special facilities are necessary in order to be able to use an individual source, for example, access to the language laboratory to use certain self-study foreign language materials, or to a projection room or studio to be able to view and assess training films, these should be described here, along with any related procedures such as a booking system. If there are personal stereo systems available which can be borrowed for use with loan copies of audio-cassettes, details of their availability should be given.

If any special interest societies or groups exist - perhaps for those studying languages, or with an interest in local history - and these meet regularly, organise events or produce a newsletter, this will be worth mentioning in the subject guide along with details of how to make contact with their liaison officers. It may be that membership of, or access to the LIS of certain external institutions is available to those who make up your organisation through, for example, schemes of cooperation set up between commercial and industrial organisations or with various schools, colleges or universities, or via corporate membership of professional, trade or research associations. If there is a separate brochure on any of these cooperative ventures, setting out what is involved e.g. payment of a reduced subscription, and what is available such as loan or reference-only facilities, hours of opening, its availability should be mentioned in the subject guide.

Where members of the LIS staff have special expertise in, or responsibility for certain subject fields, this will be essential information to be included in the subject guide. Their names and job titles, along with their telephone, email or fax numbers should be shown with the times when they can be contacted. This will be especially useful to the user if staff work on a rota basis, or are assigned to other responsibilities at certain times. Any specialist services which an individual or the department as a whole offers within its area of specialism should also be outlined. A language LIS, for example, may organise translation services, a systems LIS might arrange or conduct training in certain computer applications or offer related consultancy as long as the necessary skills are available in-house. All these services could be referred to briefly in the subject guide and be described more fully in any specially prepared promotional literature, which may well be aimed at the outside world, if the intention is to offer this to external as well as internal clients.

Subject guides may also have additional purposes such as spreading the demand for a limited number of titles, or assisting in the teaching and learning processes by building into the guide familiarisation exercises and practical work relating to specific projects. The first would involve encouraging the user to consider a wider range of source material than they might otherwise have done. This is in order to make available as many relevant sources as possible to all those requesting information at the same level in that subject field. This is often the case where there is heavy demand for certain materials and that demand is concentrated into one period of time as is often the case for students working to an academic timetable. It could also apply in a commercial setting when a long term project is starting up and members of the project team need to build up their background knowledge. It would continue to be useful for new members joining the team, but would need to be regularly updated, perhaps through an alerting service, as new sources become available. This again underlines the importance of not viewing a single guide in isolation, but developing it as part of a coordinated programme of information provision, relating to the organisation's objectives and current activities.

The second additional purpose, that of assisting in the teaching and learning process often involves LIS staff working with those involved either in teaching or in professional training to design appropriate exercises based on the use of particular texts or other source material. The preparation of this sort of material could be for those pursuing professional qualifications in the workplace e.g. an accounting or legal practice, as well as for those studying at an academic institution, or independently through distance learning. In all cases it is essential for those setting the exercises to have a clear understanding of the intended learning outcomes. The design of any sort of instruction package needs to be carefully thought out. As Svinicki & Schwartz (1988) say in the introduction to their well-researched book on the subject, "there is no single 'right' approach to teaching library skills; everything depends on the content or the objectives of the instruction; the sophistication and motivation levels of the learners; the amount of time and type of facilities available for teaching, and the instructor's own strengths and weaknesses." It is also essential for those involved in supervising the exercises to be able to advise during the process. This is where the subject specialist can play a vital role. It is highly probable that he or she will have had responsibility for preparing the subject guide and so will be fully conversant with both the range of source material available and what is required in subject learning terms.

Achieving the above objectives could have considerable impact on your budgeting in terms of the purchase of essential sources, often involving multiple copies; their regular replacement with the latest version; equipment maintenance and servicing; and the possible additional salary costs of LIS staff where specialist subject qualifications are required as well as LIS experience and training. As suggested in the introduction, the simple act of preparing any kind of LIS guide can have wide reaching implications for your overall management planning. It can also bring benefits as illustrated in one of the cases included in Svinicki & Schwartz (1988). This describes how the university business reference librarian, who was inundated with requests for library instruction sessions on business-related assignments, developed an instructional sequence to cover the company and industry sources, in order to manage the demands on her time more efficiently. Those working in other sectors have dealt with similar situations by anticipating demand in a constructive and innovative way, producing a guide which ensures effective use of sources as well as of staff.

The following example from an academic library illustrates several of the above points concerning subject guides. An important element in any lawyer's training and education is seen as being able to develop independent study skills and to know how to find out. The emphasis on this was particularly noticeable following recent changes in legal education and led to a considerable demand on resources at the Kimberlin library, De Montfort University. To resolve the problem the library's Business and Law team in conjunction with the School of Law, developed a series of self-study packs. There are eight workbooks with a standard introduction to the various kinds of material as well as a range of related practical exercises. However in each workbook these activities make use of different volumes of source materials, thus spreading the demand across the stock. Completion of the programmed work by the students is an integral part of the course and all new law students are expected to complete this within the first month at the University.

Fee-based services are often developed out of specialist subject collections, the most widely offered being business information services. What is required in any leaflet promoting a fee-based service is a statement of what is on offer, what it costs, and what resources and expertise you have that should make the potential client choose you rather than the competition. The client will also need to know of any legal or contractual details such as payment terms, liability and copyright. It is in both your interests to have this clearly stated in any leaflet showing your terms of business, preferably based on professional legal advice. (The decisions involved are covered in the Know How Guide *Making a charge for Library and Information Services*, Webb, 1994.)

If you are targeting the business community, you certainly need to ensure that your promotional material is able to stand the scrutiny of the discerning eye of the business executive, who may be receiving brochures, some requested but many more unsolicited, in the mail every day. Chapter 10 has suggestions for further reading which will help you write for business, with the titles by Dumaine and Gunning being particularly relevant.

Leisure activities, hobbies and other interests, apart from formal studies, can lead to the need for a wide range of short subject-based brochures and leaflets, as well as more wide-ranging packages of information. A selection of current publications produced by public libraries include guides to, for example, particular types of fiction, local studies, music and drama. These may be comprehensive guides to the collections describing sources in detail, or small basic guides the purpose of which is to alert potential users to the fact that there is a specialist collection and outlining the services available. Whilst not claiming to be subject guides in themselves, these often brief publications can be very effective in performing a signposting service for those with interests in specific subject fields and can act as the introduction to more detailed guides. Devon County Council Libraries produce a number of these brief guides as part of their overall series of service brochures. They are a handy size, mostly A4 folded into three, attractively and professionally produced, and give just enough information to advise the reader of what is on offer, and what he or she needs to do to take advantage of the service showing where to go and who to contact.

It is already apparent that there will be overlap between a number of the guides. This is no bad thing as it helps reinforce the message. However this does not necessarily result in additional amounts of work in the preparation of the guides. If the text is prepared using a standard word-processing package it can be copied or edited accordingly with little extra effort. The effectiveness of using various computer applications is also discussed in Chapters 6 & 7.

In addition we need to consider how the main guide will be supported or complemented by oral presentations, LIS tours, and practical LIS-based work. This is when the existence of an overall public relations strategy can prove to be extremely useful in coordinating all these activities. At Aston University the

Public Relations Group has now been incorporated into the LIS Total Quality Management Programme which underpins all LIS functions. The Group has been transformed into a Public Relations Quality Circle to monitor on an ongoing basis how the LIS communicates with its customers and publicises its services. In 1992 Aston's Planned Public Relations Programme won the LA / T. C. Farries award.

4. The user: who, where and when

Having established that there is a requirement for various types of guide to serve a number of different purposes, we now need to think about their intended use, before we can decide on the best way in which to present the information to the user. You need to make the user aware of the full range of resources to which they have access, which may be consist of several departments in addition to the LIS. For example, the University of Luton produces a Learning Resources Handbook which provides an overview of the services available through the Learning Resource Centre, Media Centre and Computer Centre, as well as those of Learning Support, Client Support and Academic Information Systems. It includes a useful code of conduct and details of the legislation concerning copyright and data protection. This gives the user a complete picture of services which could help them in information provision and use.

In order to be able to make a reasonable assessment of how we should design the guide, we need to return to the WHO, the WHERE and the WHEN referred to earlier. First the WHO. We have to identify as precisely as possible the intended audience i.e. the user or group of users at whom the guide is aimed. We need to establish whether the guide is likely to be required by several different categories of user whose level of knowledge of the subject or experience of use of the type of material under discussion may vary considerably. This will certainly affect the style and language that we use and the amount of detail that we include. If the purpose of the guide is to assist in the teaching/learning process, for example as a self-study guide, then the style and method of presentation will be all-important if this is to be developed as an interactive learning/teaching mechanism.

There may also be a need to provide other specific information in addition to that concerning the LIS and its operations and sources, which nevertheless will still be vital to certain user groups if they are to get the most out of the LIS and the organisation of which it is a part. For example, the LIS of Heriot-Watt University produces a guide designed especially with the needs of overseas students in mind. This guide sensibly starts by listing staff contacts under a heading *"Where to go for help"*, and refers to the availability of subject guides and leaflets which describe the service in detail. It concentrates largely on sources relating to living and working in Britain, citing language aids which will help in study and socially, and notes the availability of maps and travel timetables, and provision of a leisure reading collection.

User groups will vary considerably according to the type of parent organisation within which the LIS operates. LIS staff may find that they serve a number of different categories of user. Use may be regular or on a one-off basis, and by internal clients (i.e. generally taken to be those employed by, or working within the same organisation of which the LIS is part) and external clients. In an academic LIS there will be students and staff, then a further breakdown within those broad groups. In a membership association, there will be not only the members, but also the staff and, in addition, it is likely that enquiries will be received from the general public. In an industrial LIS you will have largely internal clients; you may be serving the whole organisation or just a specific function within it.

In a number of LIS, especially smaller units where the information resource may be highly focused, from time to time there is likely to be a requirement by its users for a wider range of related or more general material. They may not always know exactly what they want, but would like to be able to go and browse or do their own research in a relevant LIS. Then it can be helpful to include details of nearby external sources of information which your user can visit, with a note of the coverage and services which they may use. As mentioned in the section on subject guides, this could include LIS with which you have an agreement on access or have set up reciprocal arrangements.

Before you can make a decision on the most appropriate format for a specific guide, you need to consider not only its purpose, but also WHERE and WHEN it is going to be most convenient and appropriate for it to be used. If the guide is to be a printed one you need to consider whether it will be able to be used on its own, and away from the LIS, or whether the user will require supporting sources and LIS assistance in order to get the most out of it. Perhaps it is intended as an introduction which new users should read before visiting or making contact with the LIS, or there may be follow-up material which needs to be studied in the future as part of continuous training or education.

If the guide is to be used only on-site and with designated equipment as in the case of a computer-based guide, you need to consider the implications of this for LIS space and equipment. Whether you have enough terminals for multiple use and where these would best be situated in relation to the use of other material, taking into account power points, lighting etc. are all questions which need to be considered. Alternatively you may be able to offer remote access via an organisation-wide network, or make loan copies of the package available so that these can be used off-site. In the latter situation you will need to decide on appropriate control methods.

Where the parent organisation operates from a number of separate locations, either nationally or internationally, as in a large industrial or commercial firm, you will have to think about the various alternative ways in which guides might be developed so that they meet the different needs of each site. The email link is the most obvious mechanism for widespread contact with users, but you may want to support this form of communication with printed or other material which can be developed to meet specific requirements and which can also be used away from the terminal.

In the case of a video-based guide or slide-tape presentation the user will require viewing facilities, and for a multimedia presentation the appropriate mix of equipment. Whatever the format, users may need staff assistance, which will have implications for staffing levels and expertise as well as for hours of opening. You also need to consider what impact the place of use and the amount and type of access will have on the number of copies required.

The way in which copies are promoted and made available will also affect the numbers to be produced. Depending on its purpose e.g. public relations, general promotion, educational, subject-related, income-generating, we must take into account whether it is intended for wide, general and random distribution, or targeted at selected users or groups of users. This applies to both internal and external clients.

You also need to think about the methods of distribution to all categories of user as shown below:

- putting guides on open display within the LIS

- publicising the fact that they are available

- through the different methods of internal distribution both manual and electronic

- by external mail

- by a letter-box drop

- through other organisations including chambers of commerce, professional associations, local colleges and schools.

If external distribution is planned then the format will have to be considered in relation to packaging, postal charges and other distribution costs, and whether the target groups are local, national or international. If you choose anything other than the printed form for your guide you need to be reasonably sure that the recipient is likely to have the appropriate equipment in order to be able to make use of it. You will need to plan any distribution with the resultant demand in mind and be prepared with sufficient resourcing to satisfy this when it occurs.

5. Style and format

We have now reached the point at which, having established the need for a guide in terms of the 'why, who, what, when and where', we will have to think about the HOW. By this time we should have enough information to enable us to decide on the most appropriate way in which we should present the information for each different purpose and use, having taken into account all the resourcing implications. The budget has been allocated, we must set up a timetable, allocate responsibility and produce the guide.

Staff involvement and responsibility

LIS staff are already likely to have been involved in the initial research and development work which has led to the decision to produce a guide, and in some of the subsequent pre-production activities such as market research, client/user surveys, brainstorming sessions to stimulate thinking and encourage the sharing of ideas on such matters as coverage, content and possible methods of presentation. Sessions of this kind are extremely valuable in providing a forum in which staff are able to discuss the outcome of consultation with other LIS of various kinds and to look at examples of publicity material which they may have collected as a result. It is also useful to consider these alongside examples produced by those working in service areas outside the LIS field; you can often find that a different slant and a fresh approach will trigger off some new ideas for your own publication or presentation.

Membership of LIS subject interest groups such as the Library Association's Publicity and Public Relations Group (PPRG) could be extremely useful, providing as it does a focus for cooperation among librarians in this area. It draws on valuable expertise from outside the LIS field for its Day and Weekend Schools and keeps members up to date with developments through its newsletter. Other groups often exchange material within their fields of interest and visits and meetings could also give you further ideas for subject-related publicity material of various kinds.

Within your own place of work, the first thing to agree is who will have overall responsibility for the guide's preparation and production throughout the process. It is essential that there is a single point of reference to whom all those LIS staff involved in various aspects of the production e.g. in writing the text, organising the artwork, can address any questions and from whom they can seek advice. There is also a key coordinating role, necessary to bring together these elements of the process with other activities such as liaison with user groups and other in-house departments, as well as with the printers and design consultants. Staff should be allocated a share of the responsibility according to their knowledge and talents, in addition to their enthusiasm. It is interesting to note that such projects have often brought out skills not previously observed or able to be fully utilised at either a departmental or an organisational level.

By adopting a team approach LIS staff can experience considerable job satisfaction and feel that they have been able to make an additional contribution to the future success of the service. An example of the team approach is described in Webb (1991) and shows how the work involved in producing a guide to the business information service of a leading firm of accountants was shared. It describes the different activities involved and the roles played by members of the department and emphasises the personal benefits experienced through the joint activity, as well as the achievement of an efficient and effective work operation and outcome.

For this sort of exercise to be successful, staff expertise must be channelled in the right direction, making the most of the total pool of creativity and practicality. There may also be a need over the longer term for focused staff training, as the production of the guide is only part of your overall public relations strategy. This is why the coordinator needs not only administrative ability, but also good staff management skills. Sensitivity and perception are vital if you are to bring out latent talent, to draw out the more modest, but nevertheless talented team members, and to temper the possible over-enthusiasm of others whilst not discouraging them from making the most of certain of their skills. The finished product must be a professional one, so pulling together writing skills and an eye for design with a logical and practical approach is crucial. The coordinator needs to be able to view each step of the process rationally and objectively both as an LIS professional and a project manager as well as from the intended audience and final user viewpoint.

Writing skills

The skills required for writing good copy for publicity material are not necessarily in everyone's basic toolkit. Those that are there may need to be re-examined, dusted off and brushed up. For those who have done little writing of this kind these skills may need to be acquired. In common with other professionals, librarians and information scientists do not all have the same level of flair for writing promotional pieces. Hamilton (1989) in her practical guide to writing techniques (which was prepared with architects in mind but is equally applicable to other professional practitioners), notes that whilst some of her readers will need much of the advice which it offers, others may "use it as a book of reminders to be raided from time to time". Librarians and information managers are also likely to fall into similar categories, according to their experience. However Hamilton continues by saying that "fortunately the crafts, skills and techniques needed for effective writing can be acquired".

21

Copywriting, like any other skill, requires thought and practice. Lett (1990) in her analysis of the skills needed for marketing and public relations activities in an LIS context, identifies visual and written communication among the specific tasks which make up that area of work and in which training is likely to be required. The importance of planning your writing and managing your writing time is emphasised by Dumaine (1989) who also provides a number of useful practical exercises to help in testing and reminding yourself of the key points of grammar and editing. Other books which could be useful are listed in Chapter 10.

The basic rules of good writing, especially with an LIS application in mind, can be summarised as follows:

- always define clearly the aim of the document

- structure your ideas before writing; this will provide a framework and logical sequence for the work

- write for your audience, not for yourself or other LIS practitioners. "Don't assume that your readership is concerned about the same things as you are in your capacity as a professional librarian. They probably don't want to know **how** things actually come about", Coote (1994)

- watch your language; keep it short and simple; avoid giving offence

- refer to key tools of the trade such as dictionaries, glossaries and thesauri; these will help you vary your selection of words and make the text more interesting

- make full use of writing techniques such as tone (the degree of formality) and voice (use of the active rather than the passive form of a verb is usually more direct and concise)

- only put in what is necessary; embellishments can come later as part of the service itself.

The success of a document will be achieved if the reader is able to pick up the key points quickly and easily, finds it interesting to read and attractive in its presentation. We should always seek to be clear and concise and consider the visual impact of the finished product.

We need to be aware of the major barriers to successful communication such as:

- the use of long words and long sentences (consider the Fog Index below)

- ambiguity

- jargon and technical language

- visual distractions in layout and presentation.

Long words, jargon and technical language are not in themselves 'wrong' or 'bad'. However if there is a clear and concise way of expressing an idea so that both specialists and non-specialists can instantly understand it, that is the one to choose.

The Fog Index
The term 'the Fog Index' is widely used to describe a measure of the clarity of text. This is also referred to as readability analysis. There are a number of measures put forward by different writers e.g. Gunning (1994). The Fry Readability Graph is noted by Dumaine (1989) who also mentions a number of software packages which will test the readability level of your text.

The fog index starts from the premise that communication can be clouded by:

- long paragraphs

- long sentences

- long words

It works like this:

First measure average sentence length by choosing a sample of at least 200 words (some writers suggest 100), counting the number of full stops marking the end of a sentence and divide the number of words by the number of full stops. This will produce the average sentence length in words.

Establish the percentage of long words by counting the number of words of three or more syllables and expressing this number as a percentage of the total number of words.

Finally add the average sentence length to the percentage of long words to find the fog index.

What does this tell you? How can you judge whether your result is acceptable in terms of clarity and readability? The index for general conversation is usually no greater than 30. Based on this it has been suggested that a reasonable target is 30 in written reports or other text of any length, 25 in letters and 20 or less in notes and memoranda. Do note that this is a general guideline; for example a technical document may require the use of more long words than you would normally use. If your explanation or description would be less than satisfactory by their omission, put them in. Remember, the final judge of the readability of your guide will not be you, but its user.

Although there are a number of other points to be considered when preparing material for media other than the printed form e.g. for a computer-based guide, a video presentation, or a multimedia package the basic rules of good writing still apply. These presentations may in any case involve the production of supporting printed material.

Style and language

What do we mean by style and by language? Jonathan Swift, writing his *Letter to a young Clergyman* in 1720, said that "proper words in proper places, make the true definition of a style". Ezra Pound, describing great literature in *How to Read* in 1931, referred to it as "simply language charged with meaning to the utmost possible degree". So the words that we use and the way in which we use them, together combine to send the most effective message. When we are speaking to someone we are able to illuminate what we say with additional means of communication, such as facial expression, gestures, pauses. We are also able to see and assess the reaction immediately and, if necessary, adjust our style accordingly. We do not have these advantages when preparing a written document, or other material to which the reader or user is largely going to be responding in our absence and without additional explanation.

Therefore we must constantly have the reader or user at the forefront of our thinking when we prepare our LIS guide, asking how they will react to what we have said. When you know most of your users and potential users as colleagues, working for the same organisation and towards the same objectives, as is the case in company LIS and many other special libraries, direct and appropriate communication should be reasonably straightforward. It will be much easier to keep up with their information needs, assess their subject knowledge, become familiar with information-seeking behaviour patterns and the degree of sophistication in terms of information use. The same would probably be true in an academic library where, even when there is a new intake of students, the level and type of requirement would be similar to that of the previous year and fairly predictable. In a public library or a large membership association, even though there would be a known core of regular users, generally this would be much more difficult to forecast.

Observation of the rules of good writing as set out above, should have provided a suitable basis from which to develop the style and language of your guide. As already noted, this must be appropriate to the intended audience. If the audience includes a number of different types of user, you need to ask yourself if one version of the guide will satisfy them all. Given the degree of flexibility offered to most writers today by the various word-processing packages on the market, editing and modifying a standard text to suit different needs should not be a problem. However, if you have followed the basic rules, this would probably involve little more than including different selections of examples or references. You may also need to question the tone or the degree of formality, and whether this would be suitable for all user groups. Again the use of carefully chosen language and presentation should mean that it will have wide appeal. You do not want to have to keep reinventing the wheel. On the other hand Pyle & Harrington (1988) suggest that whilst a more 'chatty' style might be appropriate for some audiences it is likely not to be suitable for others.

Use of jargon

Mention was made earlier of the need to avoid where possible the use of jargon and technical language. Sometimes however this might be appropriate, for example in preparing material for a specialist audience where use of the occasional piece of jargon could make the reader feel that this was prepared by someone who knew their field. Jargon can also be used as an outlet for professional humour, allowing a particular group to poke fun at itself. This should be used with caution and only with a well-known and cohesive audience; it is probably more suitable for the oral presentation than the written guide. Technical language cannot always be replaced, for example in preparing a subject guide to a specific field it could be most appropriate and necessary to make reference to technical terms. The message therefore is to strike a balance; instructions should be clear and unambiguous and in a language understood by all; examples and exercises in specialist fields could make use of specialist words and terms, when the document in which they appear is prepared for a selected user group.

In a written guide which, although requiring regular updating, will still be being prepared for a longer shelf-life than an oral presentation, clichés and catch-phrases should be avoided. By their very nature they will already be suffering from overuse and will certainly date your guide. Today's vogue saying will sound quite meaningless tomorrow. Even while current, it might have little meaning or relevance for a number of your readers - not everyone will have an interest in whatever aspect of life gave rise to the phrase in the first place. Slang should be treated in the same way.

Biased language

Certain types of language could cause offence and should also be avoided. These usually come under the general heading of biased language. A turn of phrase which at first sight seems quite neutral to you, may be one to which other people will be sensitive for a variety of reasons. Whilst it is not possible to know in advance every word or phrase which could have this effect, there are several well known areas of which to be aware, in addition to those generally seen to be socially unacceptable such as vulgar or obscene language. One of the most common pitfalls to avoid is the use of sexist words or expressions. This is not just about the use of the words 'he' or 'she'. There are also a number of other words or terms which can suggest a negative or patronising attitude towards one or other of the sexes, historically often towards the female sex. As the Equality Style Guide produced by the National Union of Journalists (NUJ) states "Most newspapers, magazines and books discriminate against women so automatically it is almost unconscious". They go on to give some useful suggestions for avoiding bias by listing the most common examples of words and phrases which could offend, alongside possible alternatives. The NUJ's guide is in a handy card format for quick reference and is published by the NUJ's Equality Council. It is available from the address shown in the final section.

Other areas in which to be careful in your choice of words and descriptions are those which relate to social role, race, religion, age, physical and intellectual attributes, all of which are capable of being interpreted in terms of possible inequality of treatment.

Cutting down on long words, long sentences
We have already mentioned long words and long sentences (see the earlier section on the Fog Index). Constant use of these, especially in combination, could lead to what is commonly described as a 'weighty' style, which can make for tedious reading. As with jargon and technical terms they are not necessarily to be banned, but used with caution and in the full awareness that occasional use can be effective. They can at times provide a means of varying the style and the mere fact of the change can stimulate the reader's interest and draw attention to a particular point. Referring back to the fog index, you will need to choose the index appropriate to the style and layout as well as to the length of the overall guide. For example, if you make frequent use of bullet points and headings, rather than continuous text, even the use or exclusion of punctuation marks could make a difference to the level of the fog index. The feedback on the following exercises will help you test this.

Those of us in the LIS business will already be familiar with abstracts of text and know how valuable these can be in providing an instant picture of the contents of a much longer piece. We know how much we are able to glean from them, even though they are short. So we should have the abstract in mind when we construct our sentences and overall text for the LIS guide. If you are out of practice or have little experience of writing abstracts, either for databases or for newsletters, try a simple exercise. Take a newspaper or journal article and construct an abstract of not more than 60 words. Pass both the original and your abstract to a colleague who knows the subject area and seek an honest opinion with critical feedback. Repeat the exercise until you are satisfied with the feedback.

Another useful technique is to summarise one or two paragraphs as a series of bullet points. This will require you to think of word alternatives and changes in word order and structure which will help put the message across in the most effective manner. Careful choice of the words that you use for headings will also assist in conveying the message. Additionally this can help you to cut down on the number of words in the overall text, as well as providing structure and sequence for the reader. Both these techniques will also add to the visual impact of the text.

If a number of people are to be involved in preparing the text for your guide, and this is to be written as a team effort, it is essential to ensure that consistency of style is achieved. This could be part of the overall coordinating role, or the coordinator may delegate this to a particular member of the team who has strong proven writing skills.

6. The visual impact: design details

The printed guide

You need to gain your potential users' or readers' interest at as early a stage as possible. Before they can be encouraged to consider the content of any guide they have to be attracted towards the brochure telling them about the services, or to the leaflet promoting the computer-based guide to the use of the LIS. Your printed guide, whether a brochure, a folder containing several items, or a single leaflet, must be displayed prominently in a place where it will receive maximum attention - rather like sweets at the checkout point in a supermarket. Do not swamp it by putting it among dozens of other pieces of promotional literature concerning unrelated services or diverse events. In considering the display of your guides, you could start by asking yourself which stands at an exhibition attract you and why.

Your guide has to have certain features which draw attention to that particular publication. You will need to:

- choose an attractive and distinctive colour
- give it a distinguishing logo and title
- use a typeface which is clear and big enough to read
- choose an interesting and appropriate layout
- make it a handy size - not so small that it will get lost among other documents, but not too cumbersome
- make it easy to use.

Let us take each of those points and consider them in more detail.

Colour
You may be constrained by use elsewhere in your employing organisation of certain colours for specific purposes or by particular departments. Try to choose a colour which you can establish as the LIS colour, or a range of colours which you can use for different types of guides. Stick to these colours so that your publications will be instantly recognisable. You need to think of colour both in terms of background, i.e. the paper on which you are printing, and the text and images which are displayed.

Logo
This does not have to be an image of a specific item. There are a number of effective abstract images which will be just as effective. Pyle & Harrington (1988) in their excellent publication on designing effective library leaflets, give some useful pointers on images to avoid such as "disembodied hands holding light-pens". They reinforce the point made earlier, that of preparing your guide with the user in mind, not the librarian. Ask yourself what is likely to appeal to the wide range of individuals who make up your various user groups. Try to step outside your own role and think of your own reactions to publicity material in other settings e.g. banks, shops, theatres.

Carry out some market research. Next time you open a newspaper look critically at the advertisements placed by big companies - how eye-catching and instantly recognisable are the logos which they are currently using? Note the ones which you like and those which you do not like and work out why. Now do the same with advertisements placed by libraries - you only need look at some of the job advertisements to get a sample. This will give you some ideas on what appeals and what does not work, at least for you, and will help you judge what would be suitable for your own logo.

In all such tests of user-appeal it is a good idea to seek the response of several people to try and obtain a consensus of opinion about the features that make logos and other images effective. The same applies to consideration of commercially-produced images such as those available in 'clip-art' books and software, as described below in the section on layout and presentation. Make sure all possible images get a wide viewing with discussion before you make your final choice.

You may want to design one logo which is used to identify all LIS material, with additional images to indicate special subject fields or other specific areas of interest. In addition your logo should be able to be used in conjunction with, and complement any corporate image which your parent organisation wishes to project. Do check that your plans are consistent with any house style rules.

Titles and headings
These can be straightforward and descriptive, or catchy, but beware of the title which might mean something only to its author, or could be seen by some as being silly or patronising. Titles need to give a clear indication of what the guide is about without going into detail. They should be short, memorable and eye-catching. They should be of a size and overall shape which is balanced with the size of the brochure and easily readable. You may want to use the same style for a number of different titles covering a series of brochures, so that should be taken into account. You also need to consider whether the title is going to be repeated inside the brochure e.g. across the top of the pages, or on individual smaller items which may be included inside a service folder. Headings are used within the text to provide sequence and structure and to

29

highlight different points. Use them when you are moving on to a new topic or aspect and keep headings brief. How far you go in the use of sub-headings will depend on the length of the whole publication and the complexity of its coverage.

You may find it useful to include a summary page. The Commonwealth Development Corporation's Library and Information Centre, known as CLIC, produces a series of detailed guides to the different services which they offer. There is also an additional succinct guide of 6 pages prefaced by a very helpful summary page which lists key services and gives one or two lines indicating what each covers, and referring the reader to the appropriate page number. The guide itself is divided into ten short sections ranging from sources available to how to access its internal databases which are able to be searched throughout the organisation. It is written in a straightforward style and makes use of bullet points with emboldened type for headings throughout.

Typeface
Go into any print shop and you will be able to see examples of numerous different typefaces. In addition to choosing the style, you will have to decide on the size of the typeface to be used. The key to effective use of typefaces is to try not to mix too many different styles and sizes, and to go for a clean, clear typeface rather than one with too many embellishments - it may look 'pretty' but can you read it? Think carefully about making the most effective use of upper and lower case, italics and emboldening. If you are aiming to produce your guide in several foreign languages, you will need to be able to include the different or additional characters which those languages require.

Layout & presentation
The impact of the layout will be affected by the colour of the background and any use of colour in the printing, as well as by the strength of the typeface. This will be linked with size and physical form as discussed in the section which follows. It will have to take into account the message which is being sent and the best way in which this information can be communicated e.g. in describing the location of the LIS, it is probable that this will be done most effectively through means of a map or plan rather than text. Consider other images and symbols which could improve communication and where these would best be placed for maximum effect. The Commercial Information Library of the British Tourist Authority has produced a striking cover for its short guide to LIS services. It has bold black lettering on a white background and the images of books used in the design actually tell the users which subjects are covered by the service, even before they open the folded sheet and read the detail. The cover is reproduced in Chapter 9.

Look at the numerous but often simple techniques available for emphasising different pieces of information e.g. outlining with a box, indenting, the use of symbols such as hyphens and bold dots or circles to make lists more interesting by breaking them up into series of bullet points. Times of opening could be set in a box to make them stand out. Placing text at the centre of the margins rather than working from the left hand side is useful when showing names, addresses and contact numbers. Most word processing packages offer considerable choice of such facilities; it is worth consulting the manual to make sure that you are aware of the full range of graphics available to you.

Quick and easy images with 'clip-art'
There is an increasing choice of software which has been specifically developed for drawing and design purposes and which will provide you with what are known as 'clip-art' images. Before these became widely available as software they were published as clip-art books. You can still buy these from major commercial art suppliers, they are a very inexpensive way of gaining direct access to numerous copyright-free images. You just clip or cut out the image you want, or in the case of software select one on screen, and you are able to incorporate it into your design without having to obtain permission from the publisher. Look in any leading computer supplier's catalogue and you will find various makes of software of this kind, e.g. those from the Corel range in both their desktop publishing and design products, with the *CorelDraw! 5 for Windows* package offering over 22,000 clip-art images at the time of writing.

The clip-art approach, whether you go for the book or the software, will probably take less time and come up with many more images than you could realistically be expected to think of, or design in-house, without the assistance of a fully-fledged design department. It will help you in selecting a logo and in choosing other well-produced images for use throughout the text, and contribute to ensuring consistency of quality in presentation. By means of the act of reviewing a range of images, you can often gain insight into other aspects of communication which will influence your decisions on the final layout and overall design of your guide.

Size and physical form
We will be considering non-print formats in the next section, but when deciding on the most appropriate physical form in which to present our printed guide we must think in terms of appearance, convenience to the user, and suitability for the type of information to be included e.g. illustrations, maps, lists, text. This will have an impact on the quality and type of paper to be used, as well as the size, shape, number of pages, binding, and whether any or all of it is to be produced in anything other than standard page form e.g. folded or pull-out. All these decisions will be influenced by:

- the budget
- the availability of appropriate in-house production facilities
- the timetable.

31

You may decide to produce a brief guide in the form of a pocket-sized card, which would be quite hard-wearing especially if laminated. This could list key services and contact details and point the user towards more detailed guides. An example of the successful use of cards is that of the British Library statements of standards of their different services, as well as the University of Luton example mentioned earlier. Whether using card or paper for a one-sheet or multiple page publication, always try to use standard size paper. If you plan to have pages which open out or other forms of folded sheets, wherever possible follow standard folding formats. A4 paper when folded in half becomes A5; you can fold A4, or any other size, into three equal parts either horizontally or vertically, with both folds turning inwards (gatefold) or in opposite directions (concertina fold).

By using standard sizes and shapes you will find it easier to combine these for various display and presentation purposes and to use standard size envelopes for posting. In the case of a more complex folded brochure or one with a pull-out feature, make sure it is easy for the user to follow the sequence and to refold after use. If you are looking at samples from an external designer or producer, test them on several colleagues, both LIS staff and users. Reject all designs which would not accommodate the sequence that you want, are not easy to follow and use, or which would start to disintegrate the first time that they are wrongly folded.

The wallet folder which holds all your service brochures seems to be an increasingly favoured format. It allows regular updating and replacement of existing brochures as required, and for additional ones to be put in as new services become available. The University of Luton, among its range of guides, has produced a small pocket-sized wallet which holds a number of cards describing key learning resources services, with information on service availability. If you are planning this sort of service folder in which a number of guides are to be placed, make sure that it is strong enough for the job. The inner pocket must be deep enough to ensure that the contents stay in place and big enough to hold the full range of brochures. Watch out for the over-glossy finish - otherwise your user will find that brochures are constantly slipping out.

The LIS of KPMG, the international accounting and consultancy firm, used a professional design service to produce their guide. This was originally produced as a gatefold glossy folder, which when folded became A4 size, with information about services printed on five sides and an attractive cover with an abstract design in three colours and the company name, as well as a title "Making the Most of your Library". Whilst retaining its original size and shape, a pocket is now being added to allow more flexibility to the brochure so that, for example, the lists of available databases can regularly be updated. This will allow it to be tailored to other purposes such as putting in information on other business units for new staff as they join the firm.

The Department for Education's Information Bureau and Library (DFE ILB) also uses the wallet folder in which to present its comprehensive series of guides. These range from short guides, e.g. on the translation service or information sources for school architects, to more detailed guides e.g. on political information or compact discs.

Non-print format

If you decide to produce your guide in a non-print format, you must ensure from the outset that you have in place, or have the budget for, any equipment necessary for its use. You will also have to constantly remind all those involved in its production of its objectives, and what made you choose this format above all others in seeking to achieve them. Sheila Corrall, Director of Library & Information Services at Aston University, sets out the purpose of the Aston LIS induction video. "The video is a short programme, with a running time of around five minutes, designed to introduce new users to LIS; it is not a substitute for the traditional induction tour, but an 'appetizer' which we have running continuously near the service counter during the first few weeks of the academic year. Its objective is to get across basic messages and encourage new users to see the library as a friendly and helpful place, by presenting information in a style likely to appeal to users".

There was a time when the most common and possibly only form of non-print guide to a library was the slide-tape presentation. Many of these have been replaced by video presentations or with computer-based packages. These are increasingly likely to be interactive, maximising the learning opportunities, and they make use of a variety of media in combination. Whether they are truly multimedia or largely in one medium supported by a printed document of some kind, the same original six questions need to be applied i.e. why, what, who, how, where, when? The purpose and the intended end-user must remain as the priority and direct your thinking throughout the process of preparing your non-print guide.

The rules of good writing - structure and logical sequence, clarity of the message, avoidance of bias - will apply just as much to the non-print format as to your printed guide. Decisions relating to the visual impact of the finished product will still be central to your design, particularly the choice of appropriate images; use of suitable titles and typeface and display of text where this forms part of the presentation; effective use of colour. However on matters concerning layout and the balance of text and images there will be obvious differences. You will be likely to use more images and less text, with the text that you do use being in much shorter, sharper form, especially where instructions are involved in an interactive package. This will be more like its predecessor, the programmed learning workbook. If you can find any of these to look at, they are well worth a glance just in terms of seeing the way in which self-teaching and learning have been developed and structured. Svinicki & Schwartz (1988) provide some useful advice, showing examples of how instructions look on the screen, which should help in designing the structure and sequence of LIS computer-assisted instruction packages. Even though the capability of computers and range of software available has moved on since they wrote their book, the underlying principles of teaching and learning motivation and behaviour remain the same, although more advanced tools are being used to achieve the objectives.

The headquarters of the International Labour Organization in Geneva has a wide range of information which can be made available to its offices worldwide. Information provision is coordinated by the ILO's Central Library and Documentation Bureau which has produced a selection of guides to its various services. Of particular interest is the computerised guide which sets out how the ILO can meet users' information needs. This was prepared using Harvard Graphics software and takes the user step-by-step through the subjects covered and the range of information sources available. There are clear instructions on accessing each type of material including books and periodicals; databases and CD-ROM. The presentation is attractive and makes good use of bullet points and simple images. The guide is available in a trilingual English, French and Spanish version, and a separate Portuguese version. Sample pages are shown in Chapter 9. These include a page which summarises the range of information sources available and two pages outlining the ILO's own ILIS (International Labour Information System) referral system which can be accessed by ILO users around the world.

In the case of a video production you will be presenting most of the words in the form of recorded speech, although training videos and films do make use of text on the screen to reinforce the spoken and visual message. Make sure that any spoken material is professionally presented and recorded to the highest technical standards. You will also need to consider the duration of your video or computer-based presentation. Rather like printed material if it is perceived as being too lengthy it will not be used. Make sure that its duration is shown clearly alongside the title on the outside of its box and on any accompanying booklet. The amount of information which you wish to include could lead you to consider whether to produce your guide or guides as a series of modules to be used as stand-alone units or as building blocks to take the user forward one step at a time, according to the time which is available or at the personal pace required. The building block approach is to be recommended for any instructional package whether within a single video, or as one of a series.

The University of Paisley has produced an interactive multimedia induction programme for students. It includes not only basic location and background information about the library, but also a tutorial on how to use the Online Public Access Catalogue (OPAC). A high proportion of students use the guide and are able to pace their own progress through it. Students can choose from

34

various menu options according to their interest and time available. The programme can be accessed from two sites; the PC laboratories as part of formal tuition, and within the library itself. It is planned to seek reactions and feedback from students so that this information can be fed into future developments of this kind.

Audio cassettes have long been in use to guide tourists around art galleries, museums and historic houses. They may be appropriate for some LIS collections and some user groups. The script will need to be carefully thought out as in this case there is no visual content other than that provided by the LIS setting. Again the above mentioned point concerning the quality of the spoken presentation and its recording will be essential to its effectiveness. So will the availability of personal stereos.

When you are offering a range of non-print services and non-print guides it can be a good idea to promote these through a simple printed leaflet. A good example of this is the one produced by Heriot-Watt University's LIS. Entitled "Your Virtual Library" it uses an attractive mixture of images and text to indicate the range of electronic sources on one side of the A4 sheet, and on the reverse side lists all the LIS information available on the Heriot-Watt WorldWideWeb site. This has been reproduced in Chapter 9.

The Library Association/T C Farries award mentioned earlier has attracted an increasing number of non-print entries in recent years. Although the printed format at present still dominates the entries, there has been a marked dramatic improvement in the quality and professionalism of all categories and formats of PR material being put forward for consideration. The impact of new technology in the production of these has been very noticeable.

7. Printing and production: internal or external?

A key factor in your decision-making on many of the above activities will be whether or not your organisation has any relevant internal facilities or expertise available to you. These could include any or all of the following:

- the marketing function
- public relations section
- design studio
- computer consultancy
- printing and production facility
- publications department.

Within these there could be a very valuable mix of expertise and advice to which you could have access. If there is a strong corporate image, and related rules on house style then you will have to consult on how your proposals fit in with, or could be adapted to that style. It may be that your organisation does none of this work in-house, but makes use of outside consultants and specialists as required. This will involve payment of fees and you need to get agreement on whether this should come out of any central promotional budget, or be debited to the LIS.

Use of external consultants and services

If you intend to use external services for all or any part of the production process, do spend time setting out exactly what you want to achieve and discussing the objectives of the publication or package with the design consultant and the printer or producer. If there is no preferred external service that you are committed to use, shop around and talk to at least three different specialists in each field before making your decision. Ask to look at their client list so that you can see who else has used them and what experience they have in your particular field. Consult with colleagues, both within your own organisation and outside, and ask for their recommendations. Not only will the prices and quality of finish vary, but also the understanding and experience of the specialist with regard to your field and what you are aiming to achieve through the end product.

When considering the use of design consultants, the first thing that you will need to do is to see examples of their work to judge whether the general approach seems appropriate to your requirements. If it does, then move on to discussing your needs and asking for some indication of price. You will not be able to get a precise price until you have stated your specific requirement, e.g. for the design of a single logo for the front cover of a brochure, or the design of an overall LIS corporate identity and style to be reflected in all LIS publicity material. This can include suggestions for a single colour or range of colours which will complement the image and style finally agreed upon, discussion of suitable typefaces, and advice on shape, size and general presentation of the finished product. If you have to adhere to a special corporate colour and incorporate the company logo as well as your own, you will need to supply the necessary artwork and colour samples. In this case there will probably be a corporate style guide which you can show to the designer.

Whether or not you use an external printer will depend again on the corporate norm, the availability of internal facilities and the money that you have allocated to this in your budget. If you are making use of a designer it may be that he or she will recommend a printer whom they know will do justice to the work, or with whom they regularly collaborate. They may even be part of a consultancy which will do the whole job. It is useful for there to be liaison between the designer and the printer so that the quality of finished product really does match up to the design. However if you are just looking for a straightforward print job then you will have to go along with a clear specification. In the case of a printed brochure, a specification should include:

- the number of pages

- colour

- quality of the paper for the pages, card or board if you are having a more substantial cover

- size

- shape

- type of binding

- quantity required.

Even if the printers are not carrying out the binding, they will need to allow appropriate margins for this, for example in the case of spiral binding you will need a wider margin than you would for stapling through a central fold.

Printers are always happy to advise on the various elements noted above before you finalise your specification. They will then be able to give you a price based on this and according to the number of copies which you want to have printed. It is always worth asking about the cost of a run-on, i.e. the printing of an additional number of copies at the same time, as the extra cost is often much less than it would be to go back for a reprint at a later date.

If you are planning to produce a computer- or video-based guide then you will be likely to need some expert advice on the latest software, equipment and techniques available. Unless you are working within a large organisation, you may well have to seek this from external specialists. You still need to follow the above pattern and go along with a comprehensive brief of what you want to achieve, backed up by the findings of any research which you may have done on other products on the market or in use elsewhere. This will provide you with a realistic view of what might be possible and suitable.

Do take time to discuss your requirements thoroughly with the consultants and printers and make sure that you allow enough time for them to come back with several proposed options as well as a quotation. This applies to all your dealings with external services. You will need to start your discussions with them well in advance of your planned completion date. They will have a number of jobs for other clients on at any one time, each with a different timetable and yours will have be fitted into their overall schedule. Many printing firms will have long-standing seasonal commitments, for example, the printing of Christmas cards, calendars and diaries, so you will need to take this into account when planning your own timetable.

Even if eventually you do not use the services of external consultants, it is worth talking to them and looking at what they have to offer. You can learn quite a lot from this.

Making use of in-house facilities

The range and scope of desk top publishing (DTP) software has led to many organisations carrying out much of their own preparation of printed material. However the availability of a computer and some software, whatever its potential, does not necessarily lead to an elegant and attractive LIS guide. Somewhere along the line creativity and an eye for design is required. So is an adequate printing and binding facility, both in terms of equipment and personnel, if your computer output is to be turned into a high quality end-product. Your print job will still have to be fitted in with the print department's other commitments.

You may have to do some in-house research to see just what equipment and expertise is currently available to you, especially if you have not been involved previously in such work within your present job. You will need to strike a balance between making the most of what is available, accepting colleagues' advice and input, but ensuring that what is offered is appropriate and will result in meeting your original objectives.

Christine Goodair, Information Services Manager at The Children's Society, found it enormously helpful to be able to discuss her requirements with the in-house Publicity and Design Department. Earlier guides had been produced without such assistance, but with additional professional advice it not only looked better but was brought down to a much more convenient size. The result is a brief guide aimed largely at the staff of the Society, outlining the services available and listing LIS staff contact details. A single sheet folded in half, the final size is less than A5, and makes attractive but simple use of colour and both the corporate and LIS logos. This has been reproduced in black and white in Chapter 9.

If you are planning to do most of the work within the LIS, whether it be designing a logo, writing text, or developing a computer package, do conduct a quick skills audit so that you can be confident that the project can go ahead. If you identify a gap, then you will have to consider negotiating with a colleague in another department, or buying in the necessary expertise on a contract basis. In the case of producing a computer-based package you may need the services of a programmer. If you do not have such expertise in-house, or even if you do, you may find it quicker and more effective to make use of commercially produced software which would avoid the need for any original programming.

Unless there is proven expertise in the creative areas of image design and writing, do be wary of enthusiasm which may not be backed up by the level of professionalism which you require in these areas. Coote (1994) suggests that as writing, editing and proof reading are distinct activities, ideally they should be undertaken by different people. This is not always possible and then it is wise to try to separate these tasks by a reasonable gap of time. Word-processing and DTP facilities offer a great deal of flexibility in the production process. They generate a considerable saving of time and effort in editing and proof reading, with only the changes requiring to be checked against the marked and edited original draft, before the final read-through can be done. As mentioned earlier, they also provide access to a wide range of graphics applications which will certainly stimulate new ideas of ways in which to present both text and images in any in-house production. The pleasures and pitfalls of using new technology in writing and publishing are expertly set out by Dorner (1992).

If you are going to carry out the preparation of a non-print version of your guide in-house, then using the DTP to try out some of the ideas will be a useful exercise. You will be able to see how these would work, to structure the contents and develop the teaching/learning elements. You could make a mock-up of some sections and test these out on willing volunteers. You will also be able to get some idea of the visual impact which will help in your final choice of layout and style.

Information technology (IT) brings with it a lot of opportunities to promote the LIS and it is not necessary to design a lengthy or sophisticated computer presentation to guide your users through the services. You can in fact do this quite simply, for example, by using any of the online services or CD-ROMs available in most LIS as the basis for your guide. Most of these are menu-driven and will take the user through what is available. What you can do to co-ordinate these as a part of LIS guidance, is either to develop a small introductory on-screen guide using commercial software, or prepare a short printed guide backed up by clear labelling and instructions for each online service. That way you can save a lot of time and take full advantage of the wide range of impressive IT-based products to demonstrate your service.

As McKee (1990) says when considering the role of IT in LIS public relations, "IT assists in: productivity and cost efficiency; service delivery and service enhancement; changing customer perceptions and repositioning our image". So if we use IT as part of our guide to services we will be doing much more than merely providing information about a specific source of information. We stand to gain more than just the passing interest of users; they stand to gain a better understanding of the full range of LIS services and the different ways in which these can be provided.

8. Conclusions

Evaluating your guide

However successful you judge your guide to be, there is always a need for an objective evaluation. Before launching it on the world, do some market testing on a sample of potential users.

Seek answers to the following questions:

- Does it serve its stated purpose? (You will need to give those evaluating the guide a clear statement of what that purpose is).

- Is its coverage as comprehensive and relevant as required by its intended end-users or are there any gaps?

- If there are gaps, what are they and how could they best be filled?

- Alternatively could anything be cut out or presented more concisely and still meet the user's need? If so, what and how?

- Is it portable i.e. able to be taken away and consulted in a place of the user's choosing?

- If part of a series, is each guide effectively self-contained and able to be consulted independently of the others?

- Is the format the most convenient and appropriate for the user?

- If in non-print format can users easily identify and select sections of most interest to them?

- Is the duration time convenient to users? If not, what could improve this?

- Does it rely on the use of equipment to access its content?

- Is it visually attractive in its overall presentation e.g. colour, shape, format, typeface?

- Is the style and language appropriate to its intended user group e.g. in terms of the degree of formality, level, specialist terminology?

- Does the choice of style and language make it interesting to read?

- Above all, is it clear?

Points to remember

- Preparing a guide to your LIS does not have to involve huge expense. As has been illustrated, there are many different, equally successful ways in which you can do this. The choice and availability of internal or external expertise will make a considerable difference to your expenditure and the time involved.

- It is important to keep in mind that what you say in your guide must be able to be matched in service. You will be setting expectations which will relate to treatment and staff attitudes as well as to facilities.

- Involve LIS staff and make the most appropriate use of their skills and knowledge. Encourage them to participate right from the start so that they can feel a true sense of achievement when the final product emerges.

- Keep up to date with new technology and make the most of your software. Even simple word processing packages have graphics facilities so make sure that yours have been fully explored.

- Your guide must look professional, so look at different designs and consult widely.

- Assess alternative ways in which it could be produced considering purpose, style, quality, price, 'shelf life', and appropriateness for the job.

- Regularly review and update your guide both in terms of content and style and take every opportunity to reconsider its effectiveness in promoting the LIS.

9. Selected examples of interesting features

Before setting out to write this guide I put out a general request to the LIS community for examples of current guides. I was overwhelmed by the response and the enthusiasm - I received over 250 examples as well as a number of interesting letters on related developments.

From these numerous guides, which came in all shapes and sizes including print and electronic format, it was only possible to select a few for reproduction and to describe some of the others in the text to illustrate certain points.

Selected examples illustrate the following features and approaches:

Cover design

- The Commercial Information Library of the British Tourist Authority has produced a striking cover for its short guide to LIS services. It has bold black lettering on a white background and even before looking inside the leaflet the reader can see which subjects are covered by the service. Key subjects are written as titles on the spines of the books in the design. This is a simple image which sends a clear message and illustrates the way in which images can improve communication.

Use of logos

- The guide to the Information Services Department at The Children's Society was the result of consultation with the in-house Publicity and Design Department, which was found to be extremely helpful. Earlier guides had been produced without such assistance, but with this additional professional advice it not only looked better but was brought down to a much more manageable size. This guide is aimed largely at the staff of the Society. Full justice cannot be done in reproducing this guide in black and white. It makes good use of colour simply be adding yellow to the information logos i.e. the books along the bottom of both sides of the sheet, and the 'i' for information. It also nicely incorporates the parent organisation's logo.

Making the most of electronic sources and guides

- Heriot-Watt University's LIS promotes its range of non-print services and non-print guides through a simple printed leaflet. Entitled "Your Virtual Library" it is produced on coloured paper and uses an attractive mixture of images and text. It indicates the range of electronic sources on one side of the A4 sheet, and on the reverse side lists all the LIS information available on the Heriot-Watt World-Wide-Web.

- An interesting computer-based guide has been produced by the Central Library and Documentation Bureau of the International Labour Office. This sets out how the ILO can meet users' information needs. It was prepared using Harvard Graphics software and takes the user step-by-step through the subjects covered and the range of information sources available. There are clear instructions on accessing each type of material e.g. books and periodicals; databases and CD-ROM. The presentation is attractive and makes good use of bullet points and simple images. The guide is available in English, French and Spanish. Just three sample pages are reproduced here to illustrate the clear presentation as it appears on the screen.

The examples described above, which appear on the pages that follow, have been reproduced with the kind permission of the organizations concerned.

TOURISM

INFORMATION & RESEARCH

OUR EXTENSIVE RESOURCES CAN HELP

English Tourist Board

DAY TRIPS
ACCOMMODATION
BRITISH TOURISM
ATTRACTIONS
OVERSEAS VISITORS
HOTEL OCCUPANCY
TRENDS & FORECASTS
ECONOMICS OF TOURISM
BUSINESS TRAVEL
SHORT BREAKS
TOURISM STATISTICS

BTA

OUR PUBLICATIONS

Student Information Pack

A pack of research statistics and information covering

National Facts of Tourism
Aims and Objectives of the BTA/ETB
Top Attractions and Top Town statistics

is available from the Library. To obtain a copy please send in a £2.50 postal order payable to the British Tourist Authority and send to:- Finance Department, BTA, Thames Tower, Black's Road, Hammersmith, W6 9EL. A bibliography on a topic you are researching can also be included in the pack by request.

Library Acquisition List

A quarterly acquisition list, which indexes many tourism journal articles is available as a current awareness service. The annual subscription is £10.00. Contact Louise Hammond 0181-563 3011 if you wish to subscribe. A BTA/ETB Research Publications list is also available.

HOW TO GET THERE

The Commercial Information Library is located at:- BTA/ETB, Thames Tower, Black's Road, Hammersmith, London W6 9EL. Thames Tower is a few minutes walk from Hammersmith tube station, which is connected to the District, Hammersmith & City and Piccadilly lines, and is only a short drive via the A4 from the centre of London.

BEADON ROAD · HAMMERSMITH BROADWAY · HAMMERSMITH STATION · KING STREET A315 · BLACK'S ROAD · THAMES TOWER · HAMMERSMITH FLYOVER · A219

Editor: Louise Hammond. Designer: Terry Dean. Published by the BTA/ETB, Thames Tower, Black's Road, Hammersmith, London W6 9EL. Printed in Great Britain. BTA/ETBLIB/94/8

By kind permission of the British Tourist Authority

The Information Services Department

- WORKING TOGETHER TO KEEP YOU BETTER INFORMED

The Children's Society

MAKING LIVES WORTH LIVING

A Voluntary Society Of The Church Of England And The Church In Wales
Charity Registration No.221124

The Information Services Department located at Headquarters, provides a professional Library and Archive Service. We are able to supply information on a wide range of subjects relevant to your work. All staff can make use of the service which is available from Monday to Friday between 9.30am – 5.00pm.

Telephone: 071 837 4299

WHO ARE WE?

Information Services Manager
- Christine Goodair Ext 313
Librarians (Jobshare)
- Barbara Greenall Ext 302
- Denise Tinant Ext 231
Archivist
- Ian Wakeling Ext 315
Information Assistant
- Dawn Burnett Ext 314

THE LIBRARY

How can I get information?

If you want information on a specific topic we can search our library database to provide lists of books and articles, so that you can select the items which seem most relevant. We are able to provide information on almost any subject and use a variety of sources, including other libraries.

How many books can I borrow?

You may borrow up to 6 books at any one time and keep them for 4 weeks. Should you wish to keep them longer, you can renew them by E-mail or telephone, providing nobody else has reserved them.

Which journals does the library take?

The Library subscribes to a comprehensive selection of professional journals. We can send you a list of these on request. We circulate the contents pages (so that you can ask us for a photocopy of any article which may be of interest), or you can see the whole journal.

Research

We have access to external databases which enable us to help with research, providing detailed UK, European and international business reporting along with

Reproduced by kind permission of the Childrens Society

46

company information and market research. We are also able to supply the complete text of articles from many national newspapers, give details of books held by the British Library, and access details of research projects currently being undertaken by other voluntary agencies.

Reference Collection

You can look up facts, figures, addresses, spelling! - and much more in the reference collection which includes train timetables, maps, accommodation guides, dictionaries, encyclopedias and statistics. We will consult our reference books for you if you are not based at HQ.

New additions to the library

For an update of items recently added to library stock please refer to the list which appears on E-Mail at the end of each month. All these items are available for loan.

New development

We hope that our Library Database will be available for you to search on your own computer in the near future.

THE ARCHIVE

The Archive contains records - documents, files, photographs and publications - that chart the work of The Children's Society since it was founded in 1881 through to the present day.

What's in the Archive?

The records cover every aspect of the Society's work including social work policies and practice, social work projects, former children's homes, committee and working party papers; Society appeals and fundraising campaigns, including publicity and policy; major publications such as the former supporter magazines 'Our Waifs and Strays' (1882-1952), 'Gateway' (1953-1993) and Annual Reports from 1882. We also have an extensive collection of 10,000 archive photographs dating from the nineteenth century.

Why the Archive needs your records

Today's records are the historical documents of the future, recording the Society's policy decisions, working practices and information about research it has

initiated. It is important that current records, files and photographs from all areas of the Society are transferred to the Archive for safe keeping. Please do not destroy material without first contacting the Archivist, who is also able to visit offices and projects to give advice on record retention and the transfer of material to the Archive.

Information can still be obtained from files by depositors once records have been transferred to the Archive. Staff depositing files are also able to place access restrictions on their records.

What can I find out from the Archive?

The Archivist can answer enquiries about the Society's history and recent development. In addition, picture research can be undertaken on the archive photograph collection. Copy prints can be made, prices available on application.

How can I make the Society's history work for me?

The Archive offers you the means to let the public know about the innovative work the Society has been doing for over a hundred years.

A **History Booklet** entitled 'Making Lives Worth Living Since 1881' outlines the Society's history and is available direct from the Luton Warehouse.

An attractive **History Exhibition** showing the development of the Society to the present day is available for use at major exhibitions and events. Material relating to other aspects of the Society can also be provided for use in displays.

A **Slide Pack** consisting of 30 slides taken from a selection of archive photographs and documents comes complete with a commentary text. Packs can be either borrowed or purchased.

A **Schools Pack** for use in schools by Appeals Organisers and teachers is being developed. In the meantime a Spotlight pack with posters, history sheet and questions for use in class can be obtained from the Archive.

The Children's Society

The Children's Society, Edward Rudolf House, Margery Street, London WC1X 0JL
PA9034

Reproduced by kind permission of the Childrens Society

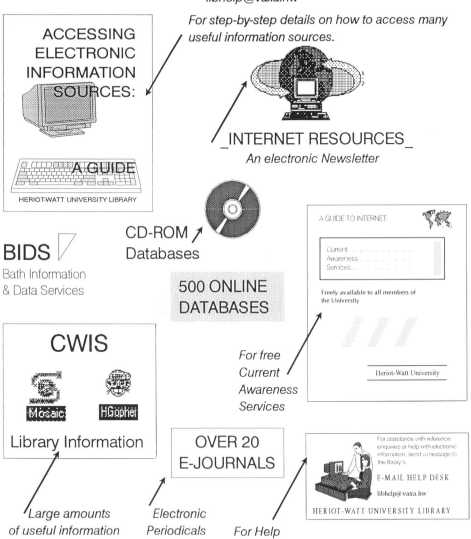

YOUR VIRTUAL LIBRARY

For more information about any of these services, contact ext 3582 or e-mail
libhelp@vaxa.hw

*For step-by-step details on how to access many
useful information sources.*

ACCESSING
ELECTRONIC
INFORMATION
SOURCES:

A GUIDE

HERIOT-WATT UNIVERSITY LIBRARY

INTERNET RESOURCES
An electronic Newsletter

CD-ROM
Databases

BIDS
Bath Information
& Data Services

500 ONLINE
DATABASES

A GUIDE TO INTERNET:

Current . . . .
Awareness . . . .
Services . . . .

Freely available to all members of
the University

Heriot-Watt University

CWIS

Mosaic   HGopher

Library Information

*For free
Current
Awareness
Services*

OVER 20
E-JOURNALS

For assistance with reference
enquiries or help with electronic
information, send a message to
the library's

E-MAIL HELP DESK
libhelp@vaxa.hw

HERIOT-WATT UNIVERSITY LIBRARY

*Large amounts
of useful information*

*Electronic
Periodicals*

For Help

HERIOT-WATT UNIVERSITY LIBRARY

By kind permission of Heriot-Watt University

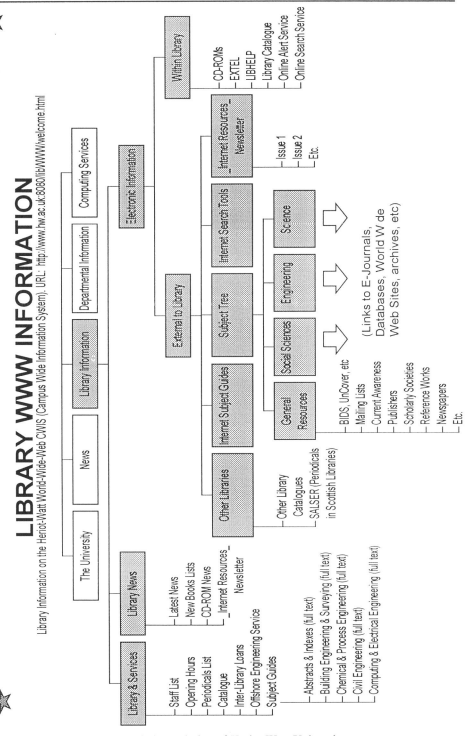

By kind permission of Heriot Watt University

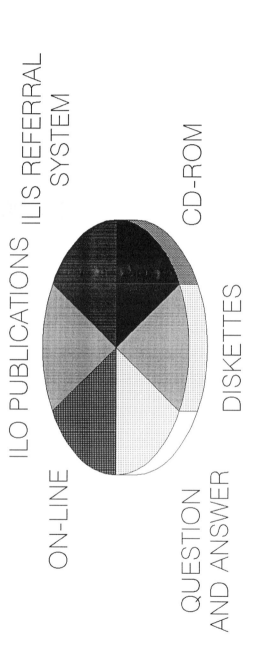

How can you access
ILO information?

ILIS REFERRAL SYSTEM

CD-ROM

ILO PUBLICATIONS

DISKETTES

ON-LINE

QUESTION AND ANSWER

By kind permission of the International Labour Organization

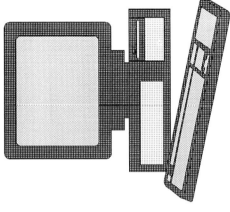

ACCESSING ILO INFORMATION

ILIS Referral System

A Menu–Driven Computer System providing Access to:

- ILO Databases

- A Directory of ILO Information

By kind permission of the International Labour Organization

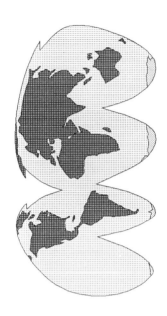

ACCESSING ILO INFORMATION

ILIS Referral System

A computerized access system, available to:

- ILO Constituents

- ILO Offices

By kind permission of the International Labour Organization

10. Further reading

BS 5261C:1976 (1976) - Marks for copy preparation and proof correction. London: British Standards Institution

Coote, H (1994) How to market your library service effectively. London: Aslib

Dorner, J (1992) Writing on disk: An A-Z handbook of terms, tips and techniques for authors and publishers. Stevenage: John Taylor Book Ventures

Dumaine, D (1989) Write to the top: writing for corporate success. NY: Random House

Dummett, M (1993) Grammar and style. London: Duckworth

Gunning, R (1994) How to take the fog out of business writing. USA: Dartnell

Hamilton, A (1989) Writing matters. London: RIBA Publications

Hamilton, F (1990) Infopromotion. Aldershot: Gower

Lett, B (1990) Training for marketing and public relations in libraries. *Chapter in Handbook of library training practice Vol.2. edited by Prytherch, R.* Aldershot: Gower

McKee, B (1990) New technology and the PR challenge for libraries. *Proceedings of the 1989 PPRG weekend school, edited by Coleman, D & Pyle, J.* Sheffield: Publicity & Public Relations Group of the Library Association

Marshall, J & Macdonald, F *editors* (1994) Questions of English. Oxford: OUP

Pyle, J & Harrington, S (1988) Making leaflets work: the librarian's guide to effective publicity. Sheffield: Publicity & Public Relations Group of the Library Association

Sadgrove, K (1991) Writing to sell: the complete guide to copywriting for business. London: Robert Hale

Svinicki, M & Schwartz, B A (1988) Designing instruction for library users: a practical guide. NY: Marcel Dekker

Webb, S P (1988) Creating an information service, 2nd edition. London: Aslib

Webb, S P (1994) Making a charge for library and information services. London: Aslib

Webb, S P (1991) Personal development in information work, 2nd edition. London: Aslib

11. Organisations and addresses

1. For information on the Library Association/T C Farries P R awards:

Contact: Lorna Maitland (PR Awards)
T J Farries & Co. Ltd.
Library supplier of books and multimedia
Irongray Road
Lochside
Dumfries DG2 0LH
Tel: 01387-720755

2. To obtain a copy of the Equality Style Guide:

Contact: National Union of Journalists Equality Council
314-320 Grays Inn Road
London WC1X 8DP
Tel: 0171-278 7916

3. For details of the Publicity and Public Relations Group of the Library Association:

Contact: Linda Farnworth
Honorary Secretary
118 Springmeadow
Clayton-Le-Woods
Leyland
Lancs PR5 2LY
Tel: 01772-39775

4. General information, consultancy and training:

Aslib, The Association for Information Management
Information House
20-24 Old Street
London EC1V 9AP
Tel: 0171 253 4488

Although Aslib has no formal PR subject interest group, it has considerable interest in this area and can advise through its consultancy, information and training departments.